MEET THE TEACHER

By Joyce Jeffries

Gareth Stevens
Publishing

Please visit our website, www.garethstevens.com. For a free color catalog of all our high-quality books, call toll free 1-800-542-2595 or fax 1-877-542-2596.

Library of Congress Cataloging-in-Publication Data

Jeffries, Joyce.
  Meet the teacher / Joyce Jeffries.
      p. cm. — (People around town)
  Includes index.
  ISBN 978-1-4339-7341-3 (pbk.)
  ISBN 978-1-4339-7342-0 (6-pack)
  ISBN 978-1-4339-7340-6 (library binding)
  1. Teachers—Juvenile literature. I. Title.
  LB1775.J44 2013
  371.1—dc23

                                        2012008302

First Edition

Published in 2013 by
Gareth Stevens Publishing
111 East 14th Street, Suite 349
New York, NY 10003

Editor: Katie Kawa
Designer: Andrea Davison-Bartolotta

Photo credits: Cover, pp. 13, 19, 24 (library) Digital Vision/Thinkstock; p. 1 Hemera/Thinkstock; p. 5 iStockphoto/Thinkstock; p. 7 Brand X Pictures/Thinkstock; pp. 9, 24 (pencil) Juriah Mosin/Shutterstock.com; p. 11 Creatas/Thinkstock; pp. 15, 17, 24 (chalkboards) Photodisc/Thinkstock; p. 21 Nadejda Ivanova/Shutterstock.com; p. 23 Wavebreak Media/Thinkstock.

Printed in the United States of America

CPSIA compliance information: Batch #CS12GS: For further information contact Gareth Stevens, New York, New York at 1-800-542-2595.

Contents

A teacher works
with a group of kids.
This is her class.

She helps them write new words.

They write with pencils.

She helps them read books too.

They go to a place
with a lot of books.
This is a library.

Teachers use maps. These show different places on Earth.

They write on boards.
These are called
chalkboards.

apple
ant
atom
anim
airplane

17

There are many kinds
of teachers.

Some teach about the past. This is called history.

21

Some teach math.
They help kids add.

2 + 1 = 3

2 + 2 = 4

2 + 3 = 5

23

Words to Know

chalkboard library pencil

Index